MONSTER TRUCK

FOR KIDS AGES +3

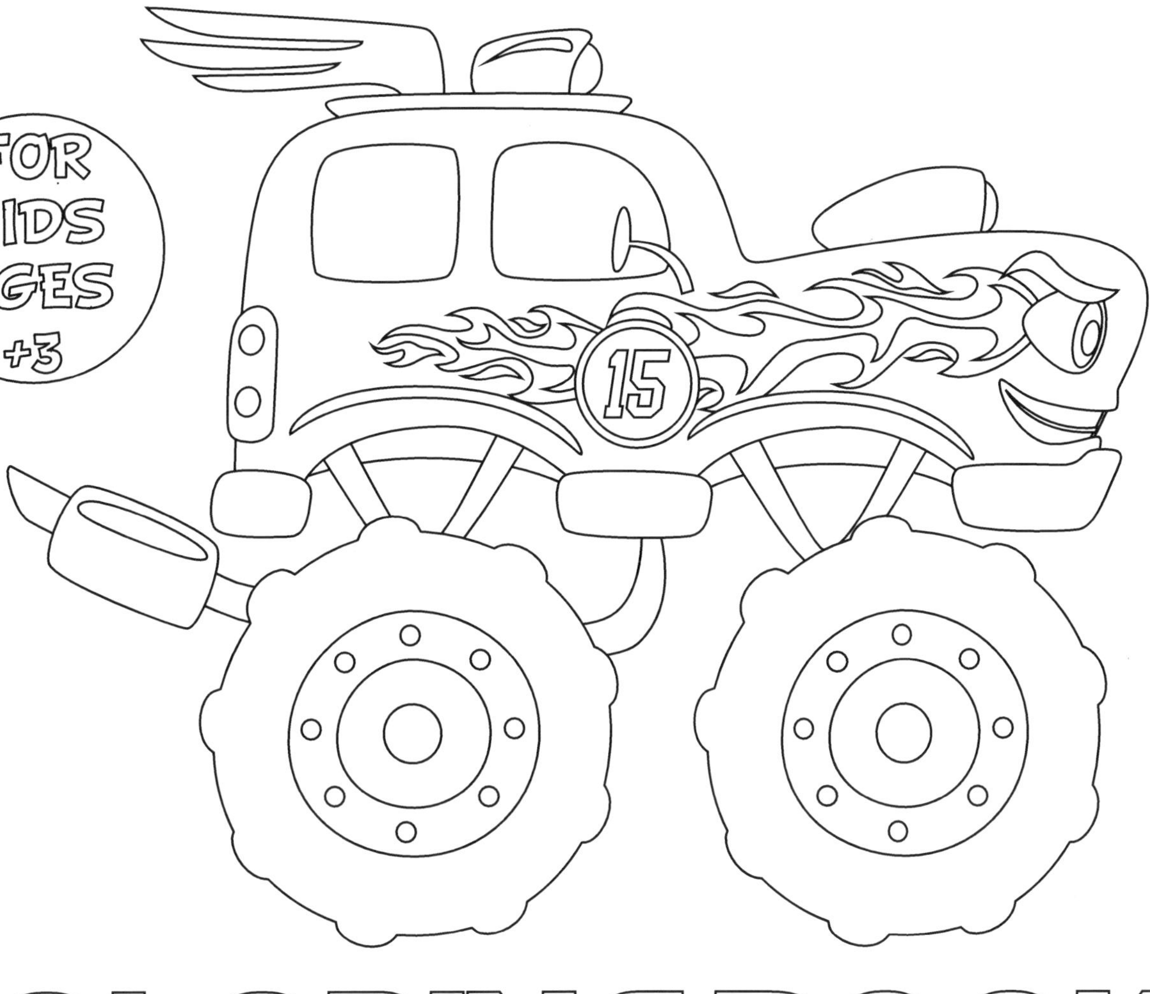

COLORING BOOK

MONSTER TRUCK

THIS COLORING BOOK BELONGS TO:

____

____

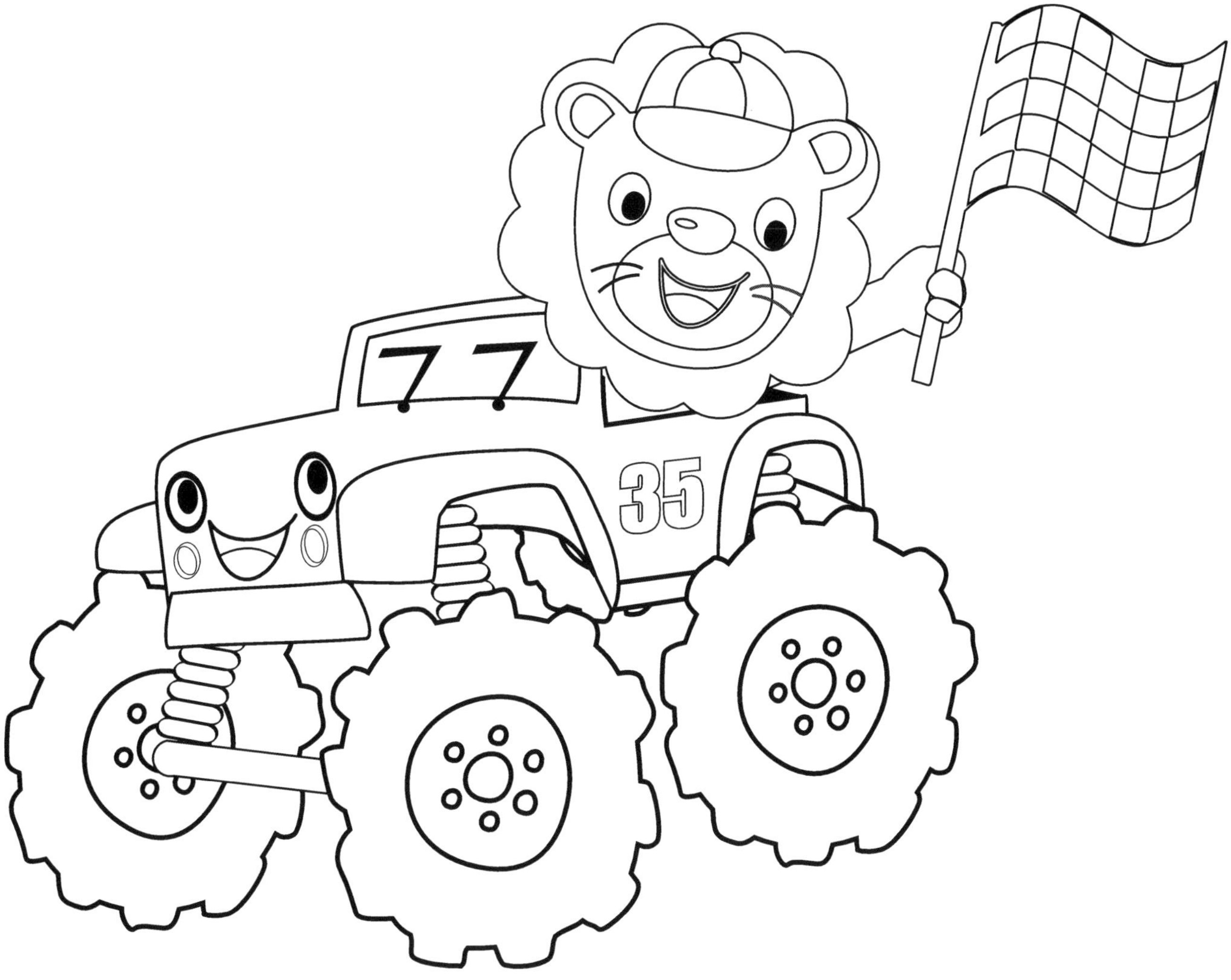
77
35

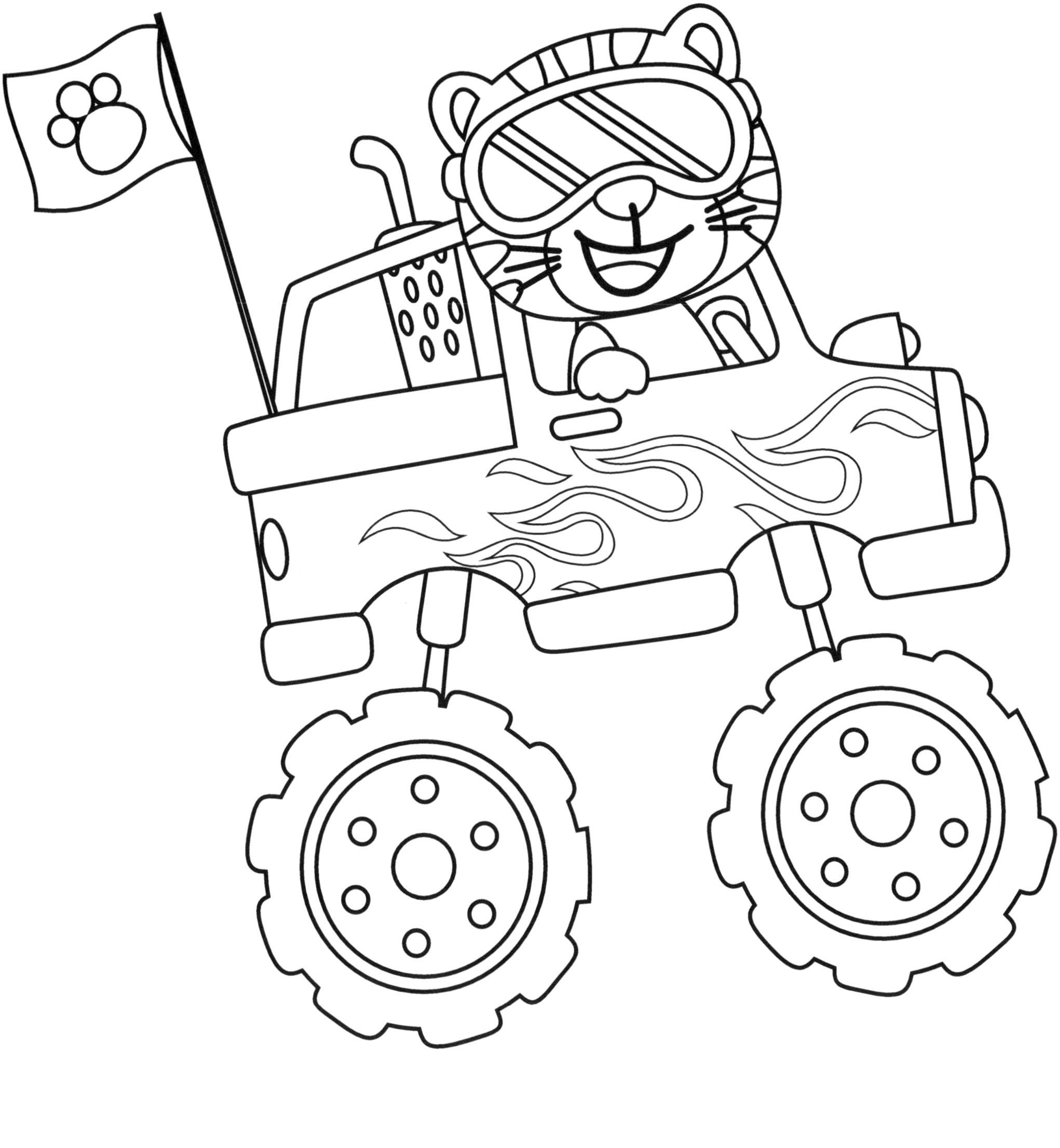

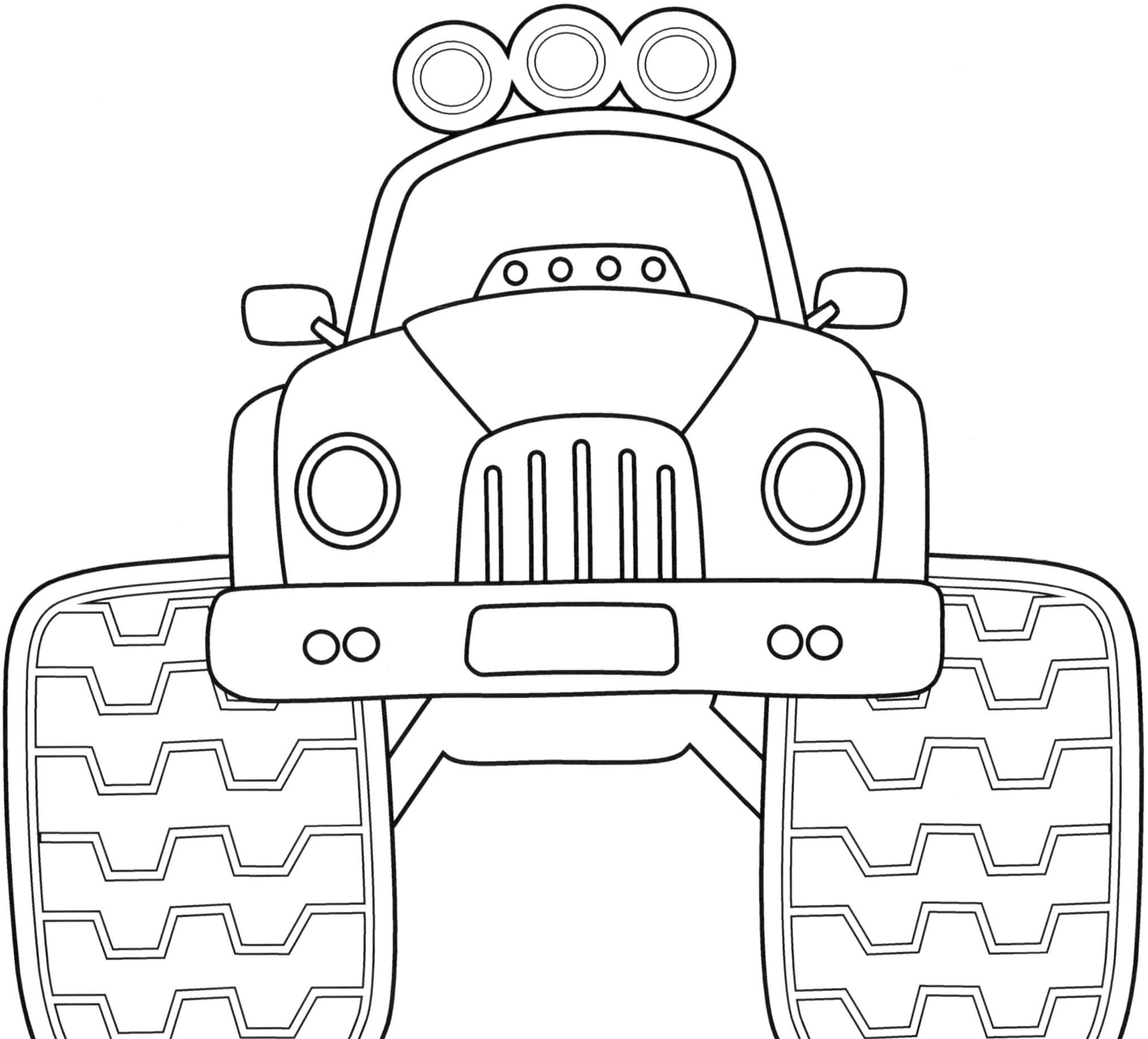

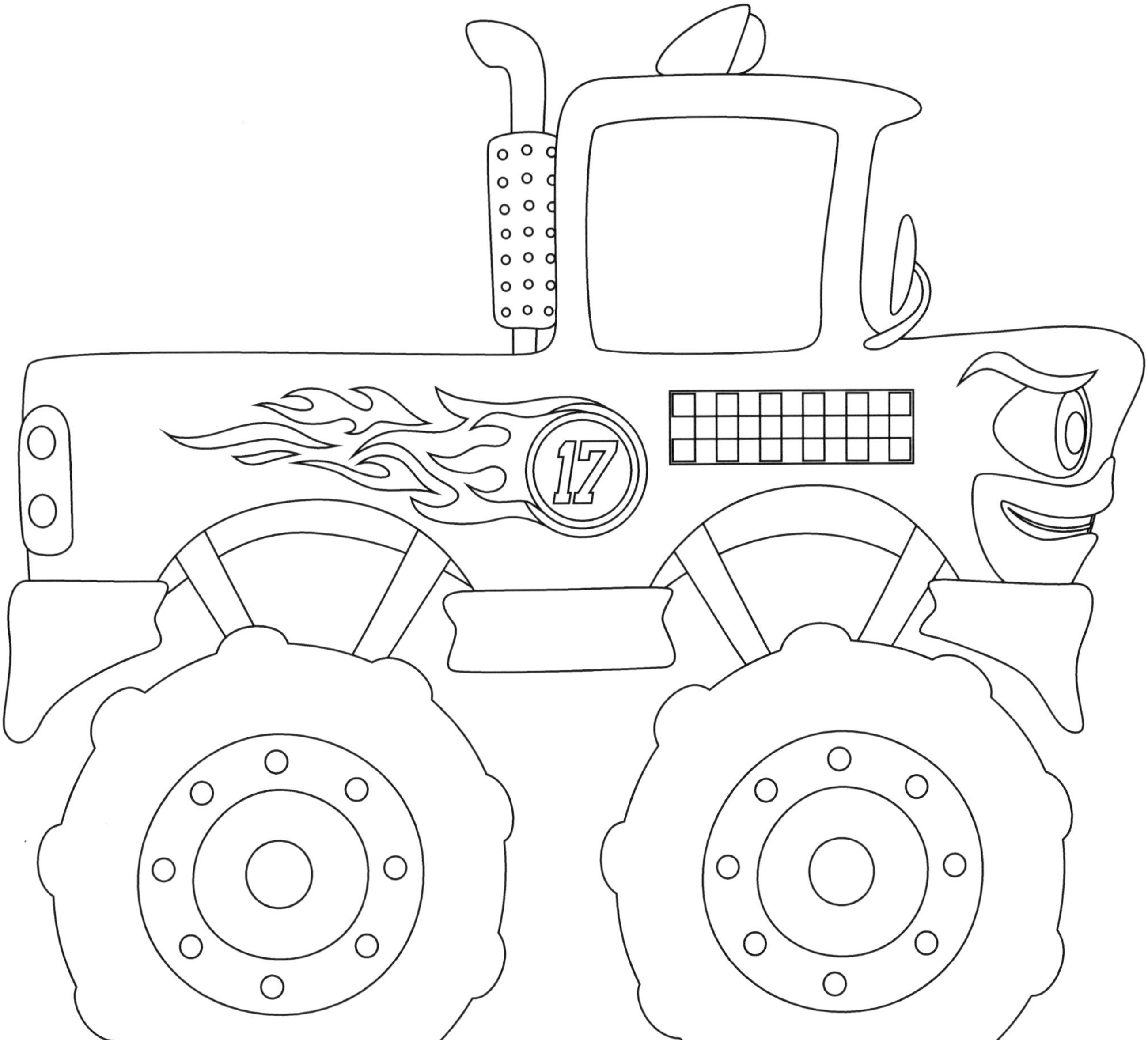
17

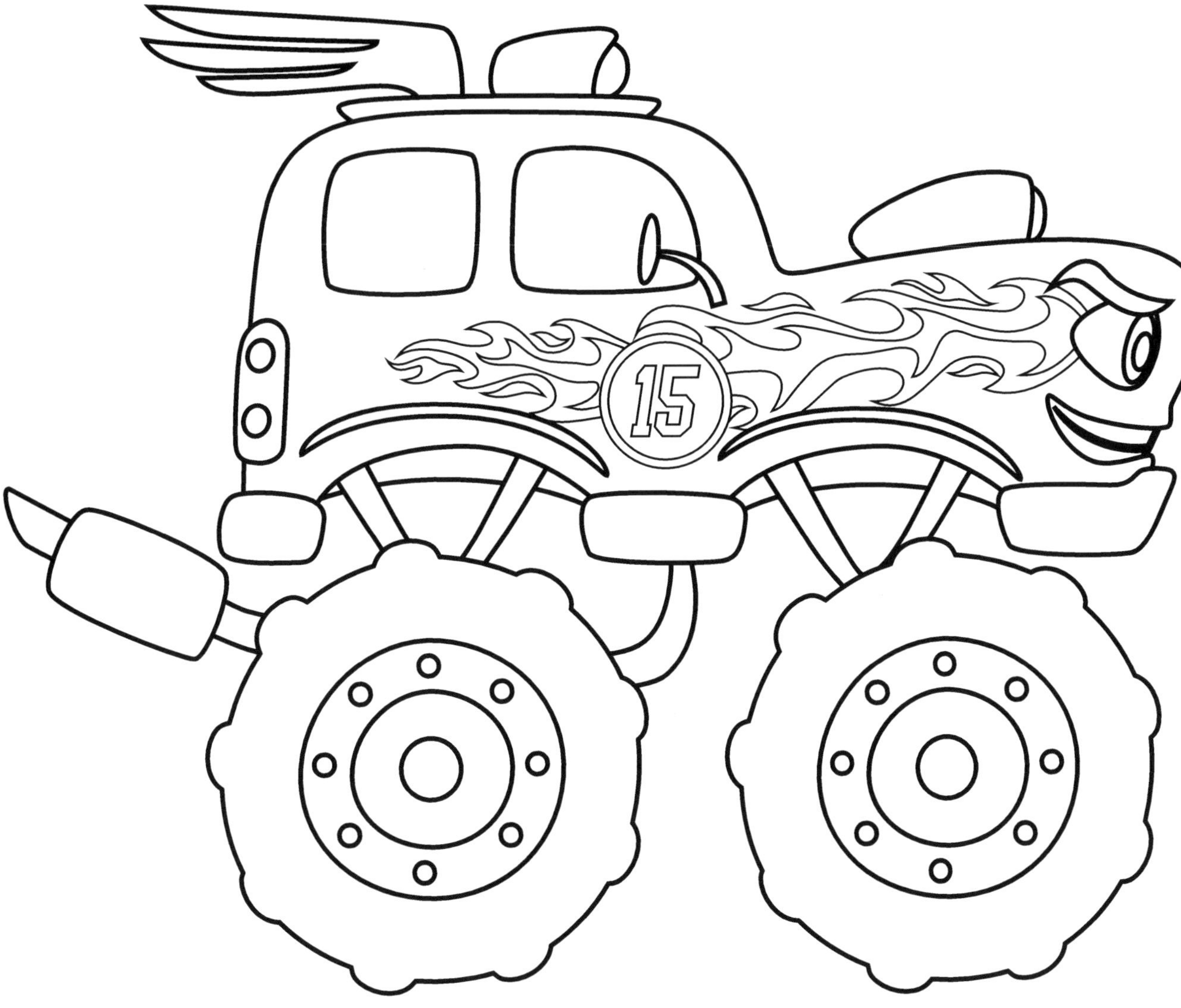
15

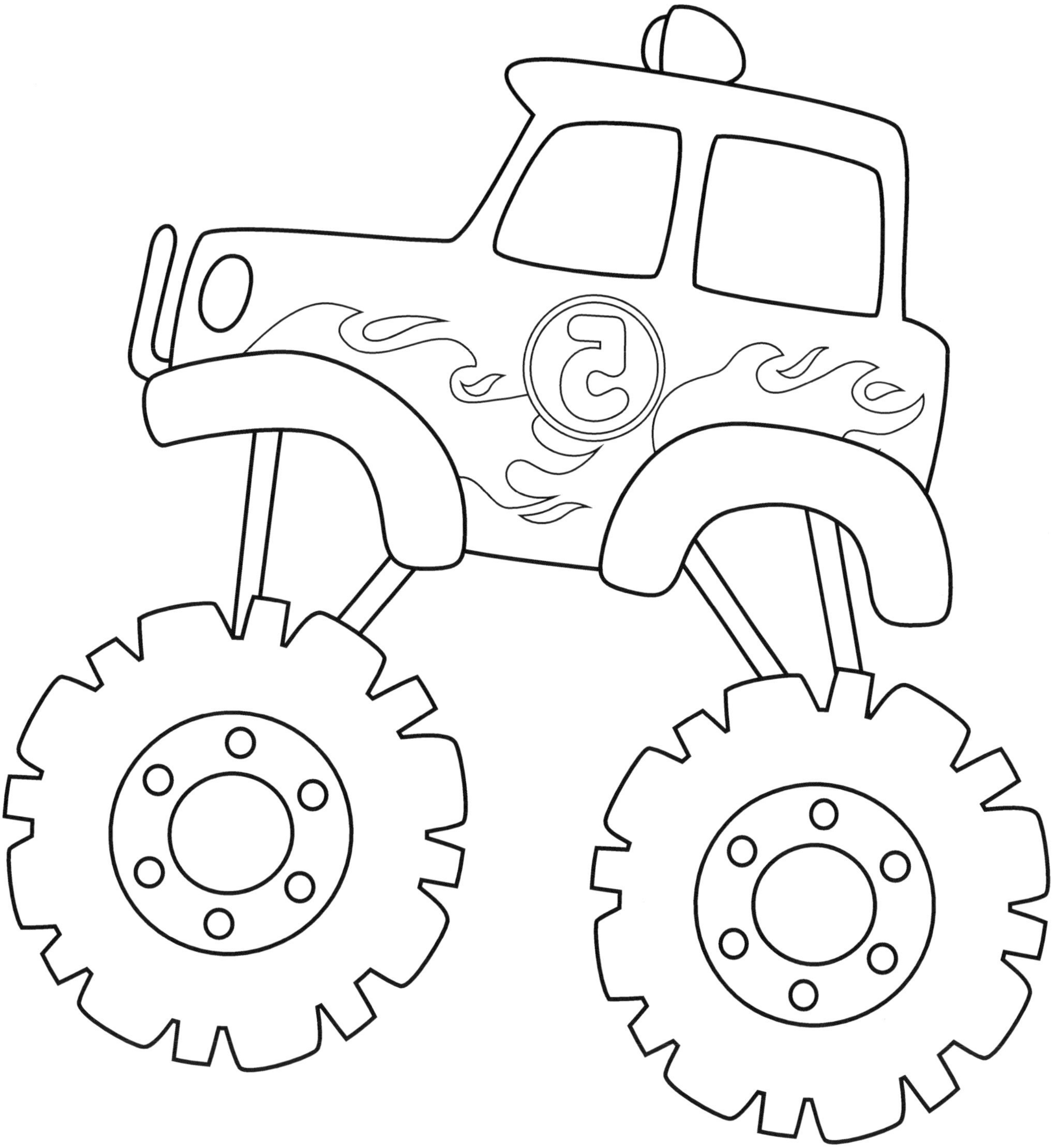
5

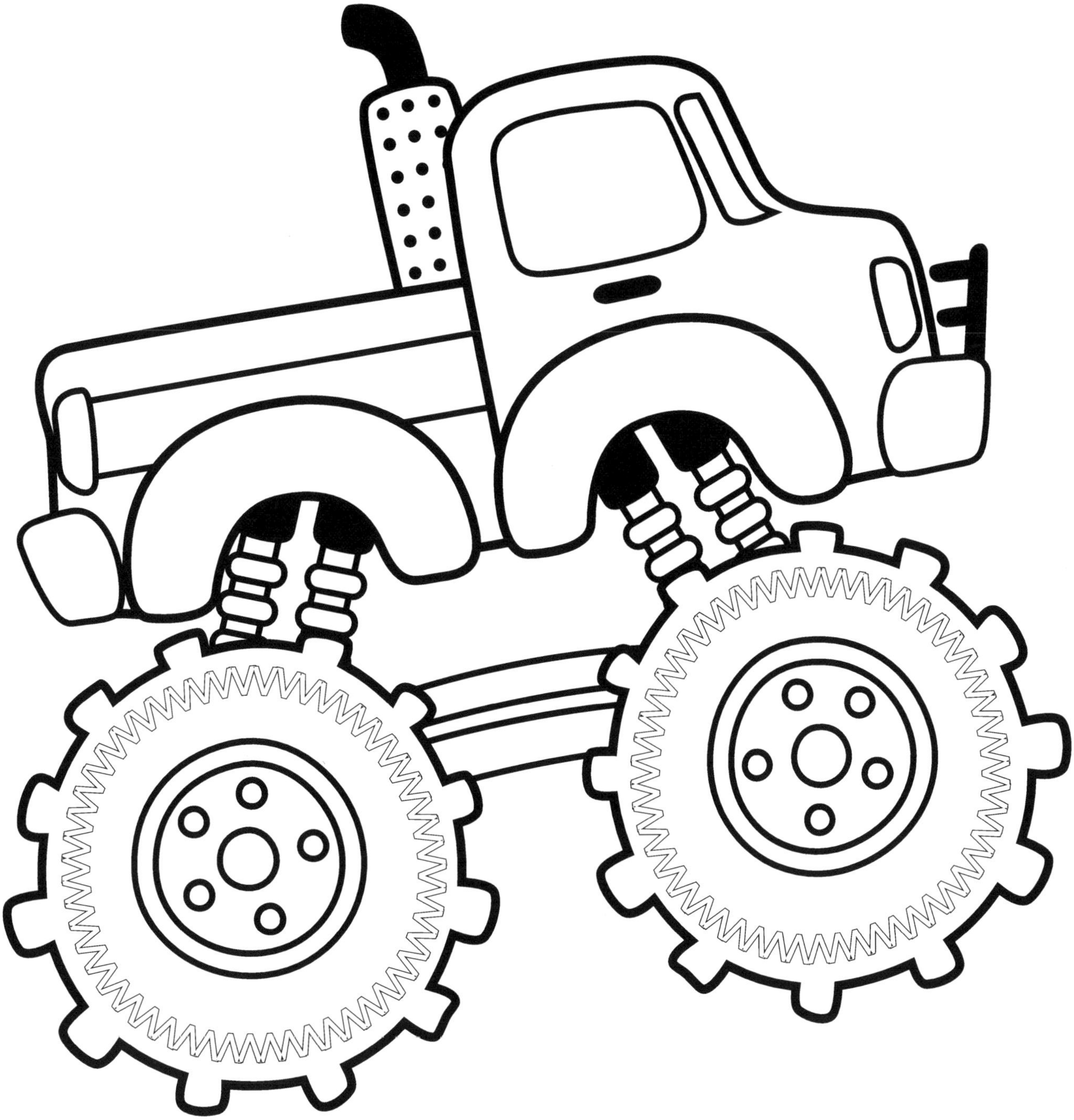

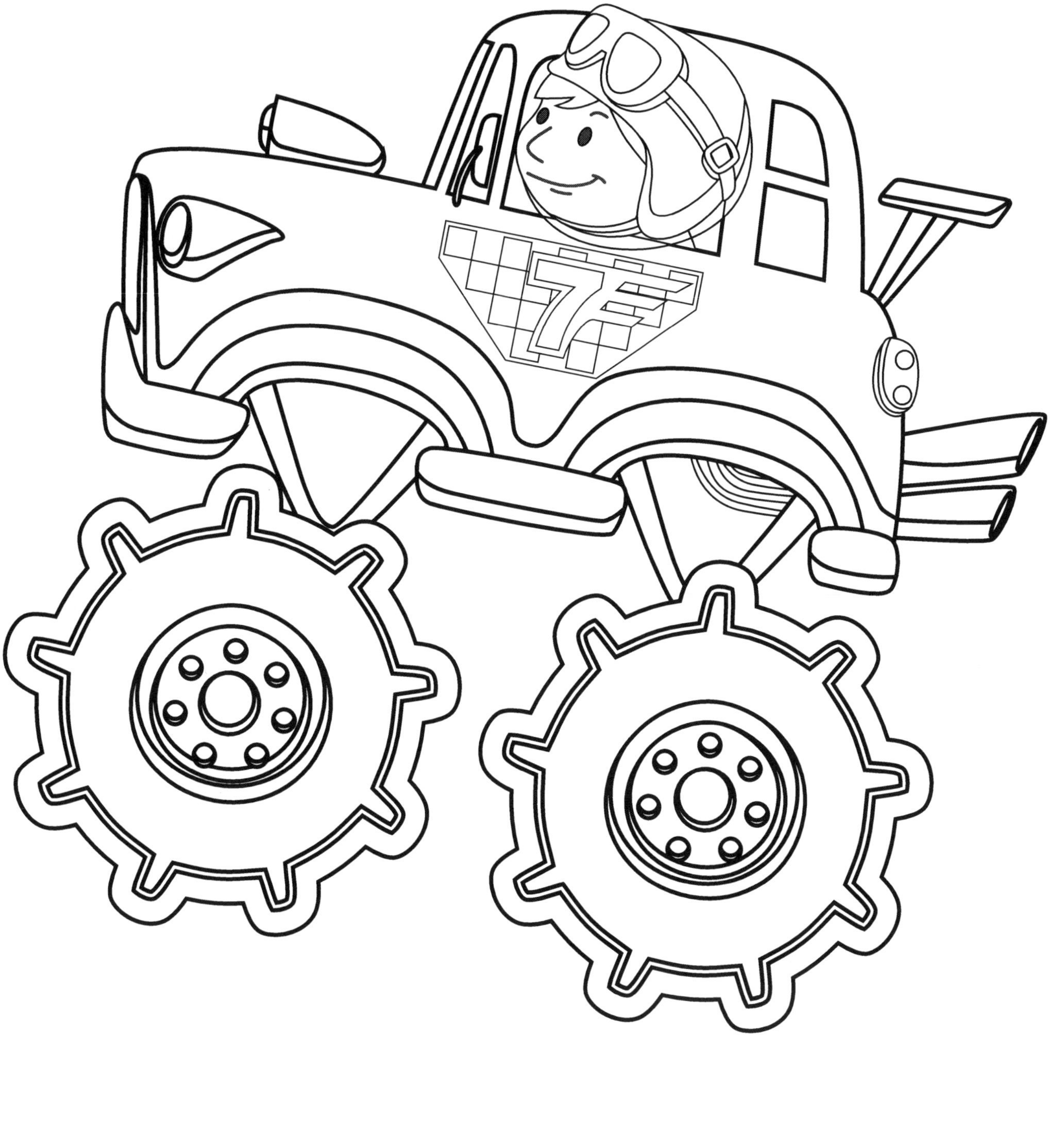
7

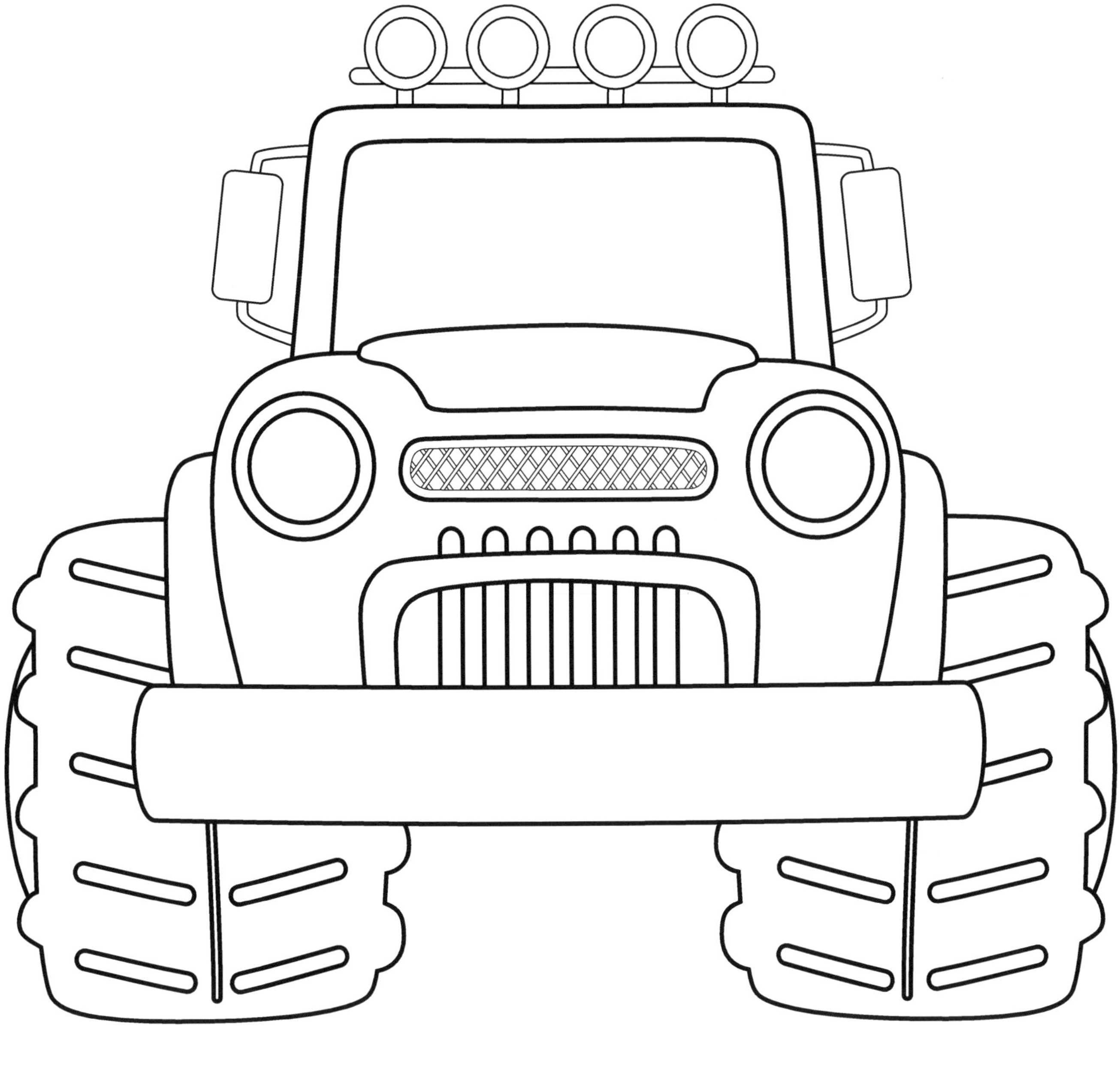

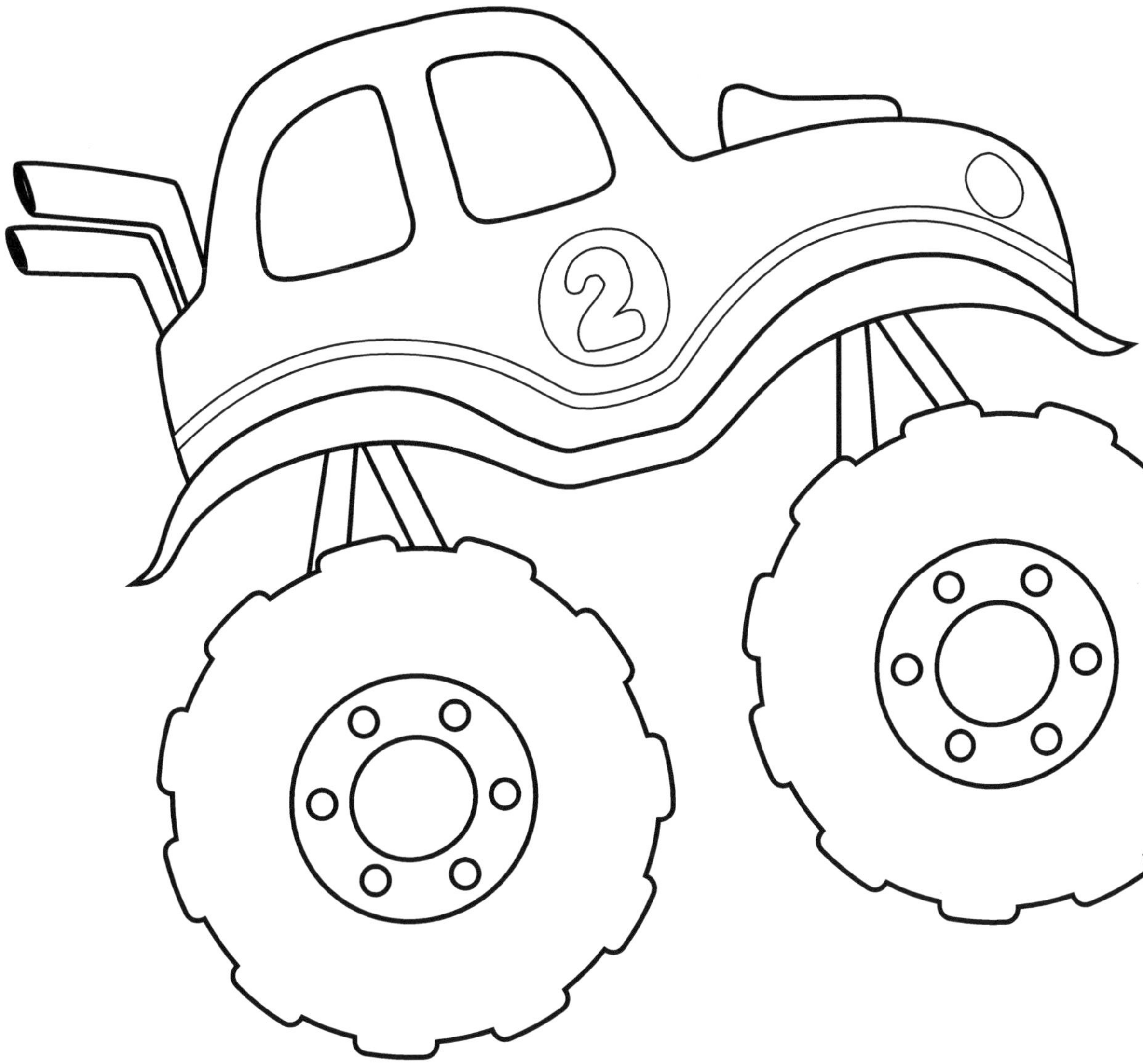
2

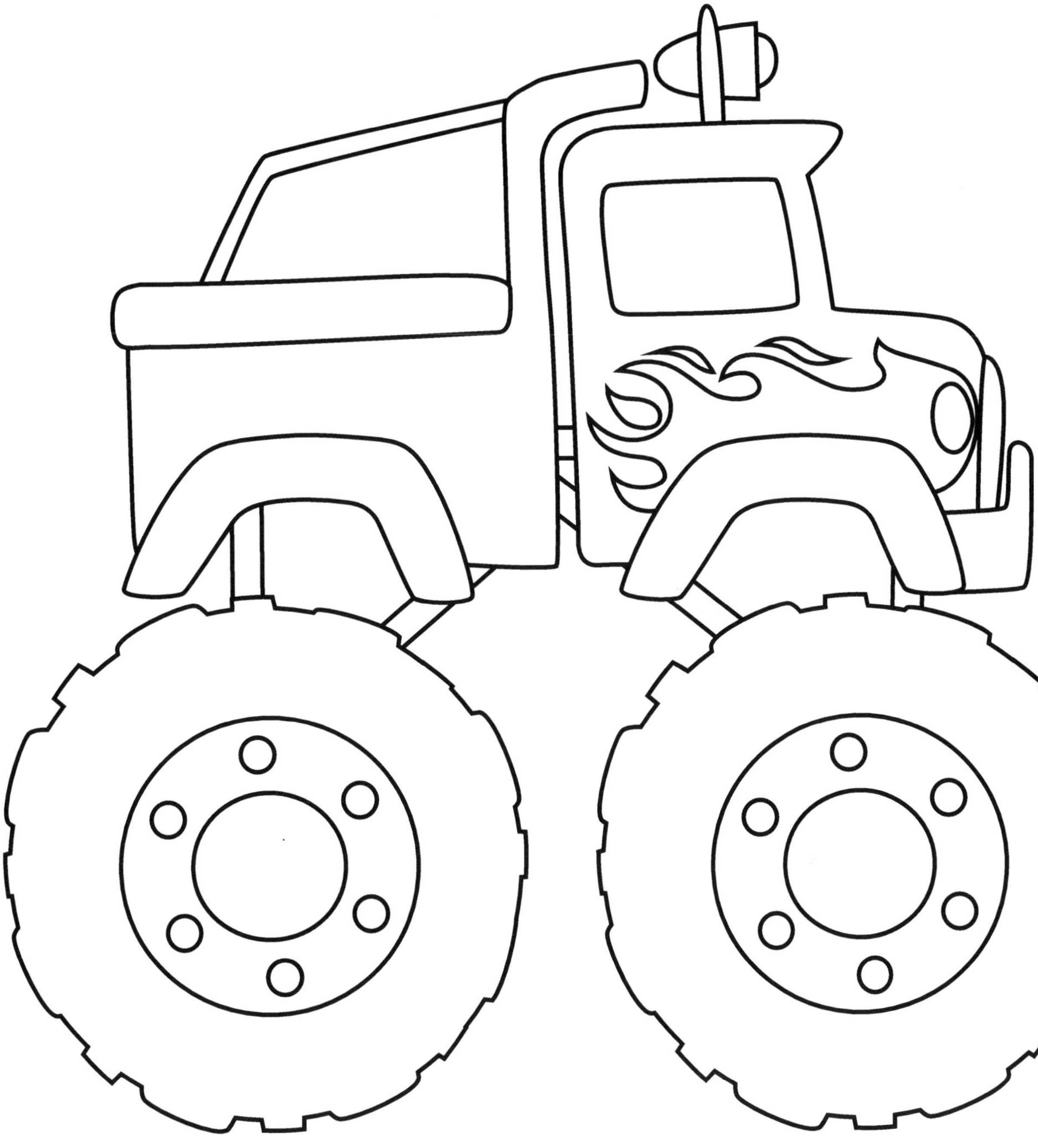

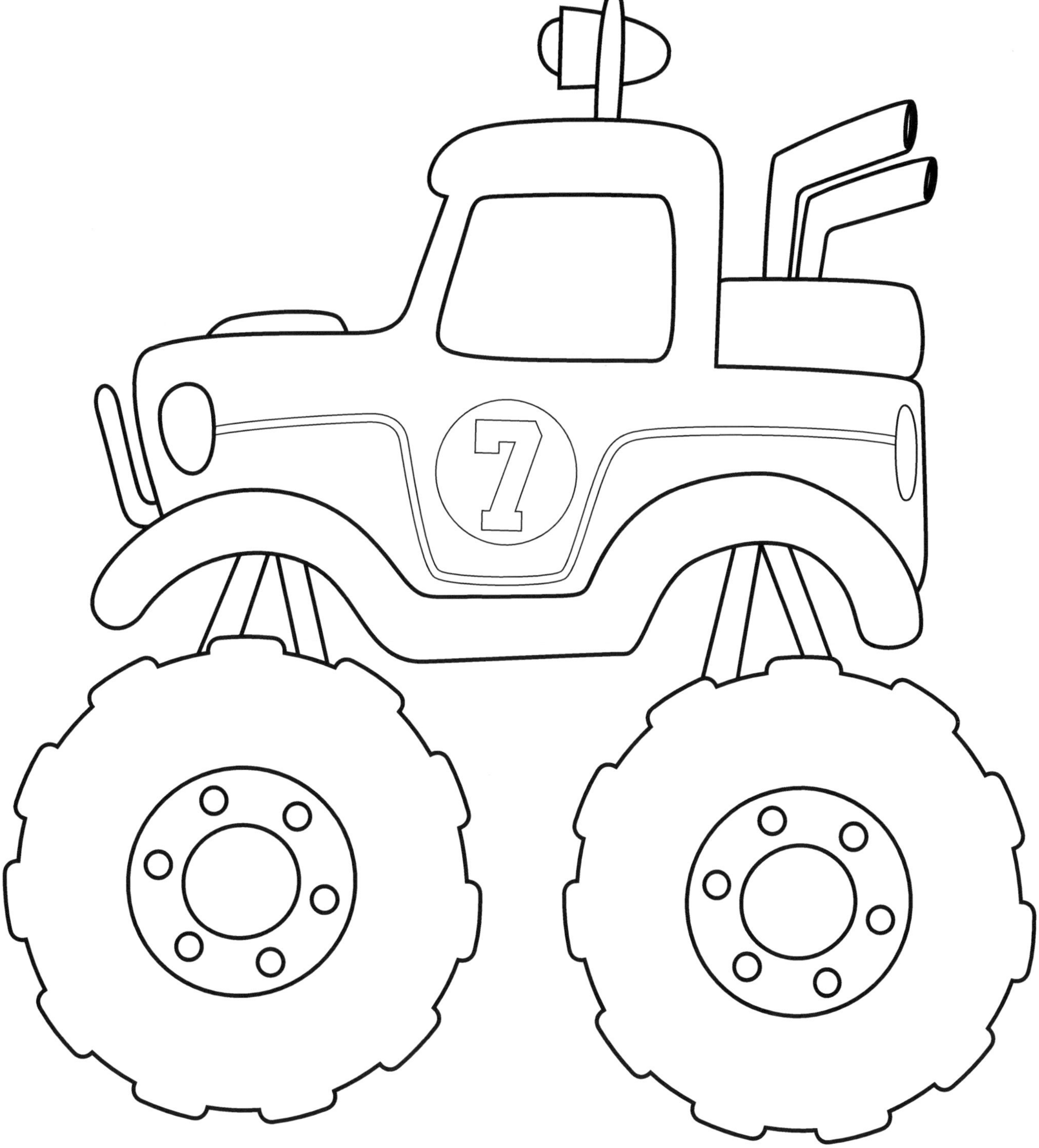
7

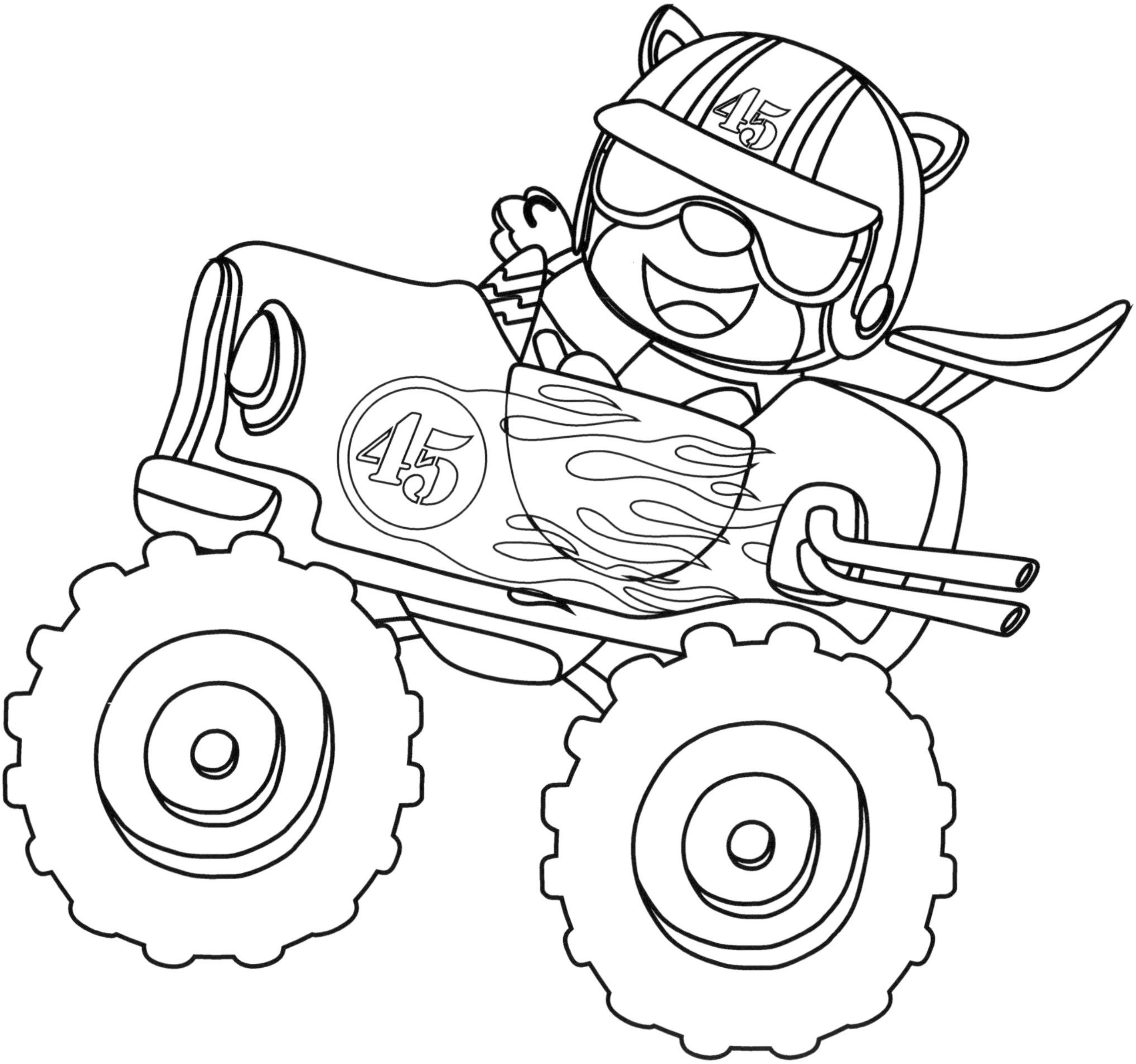
45
45

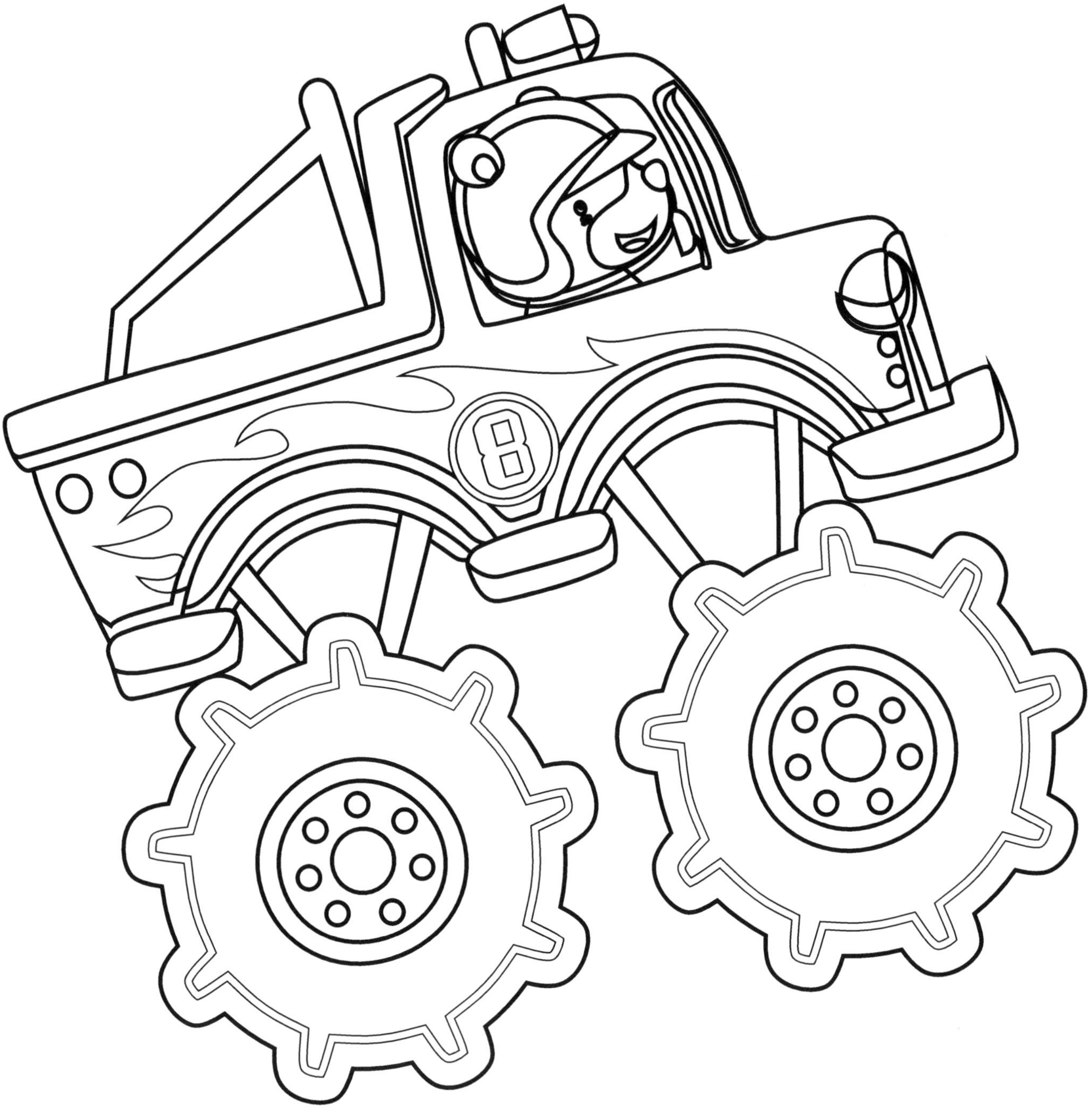

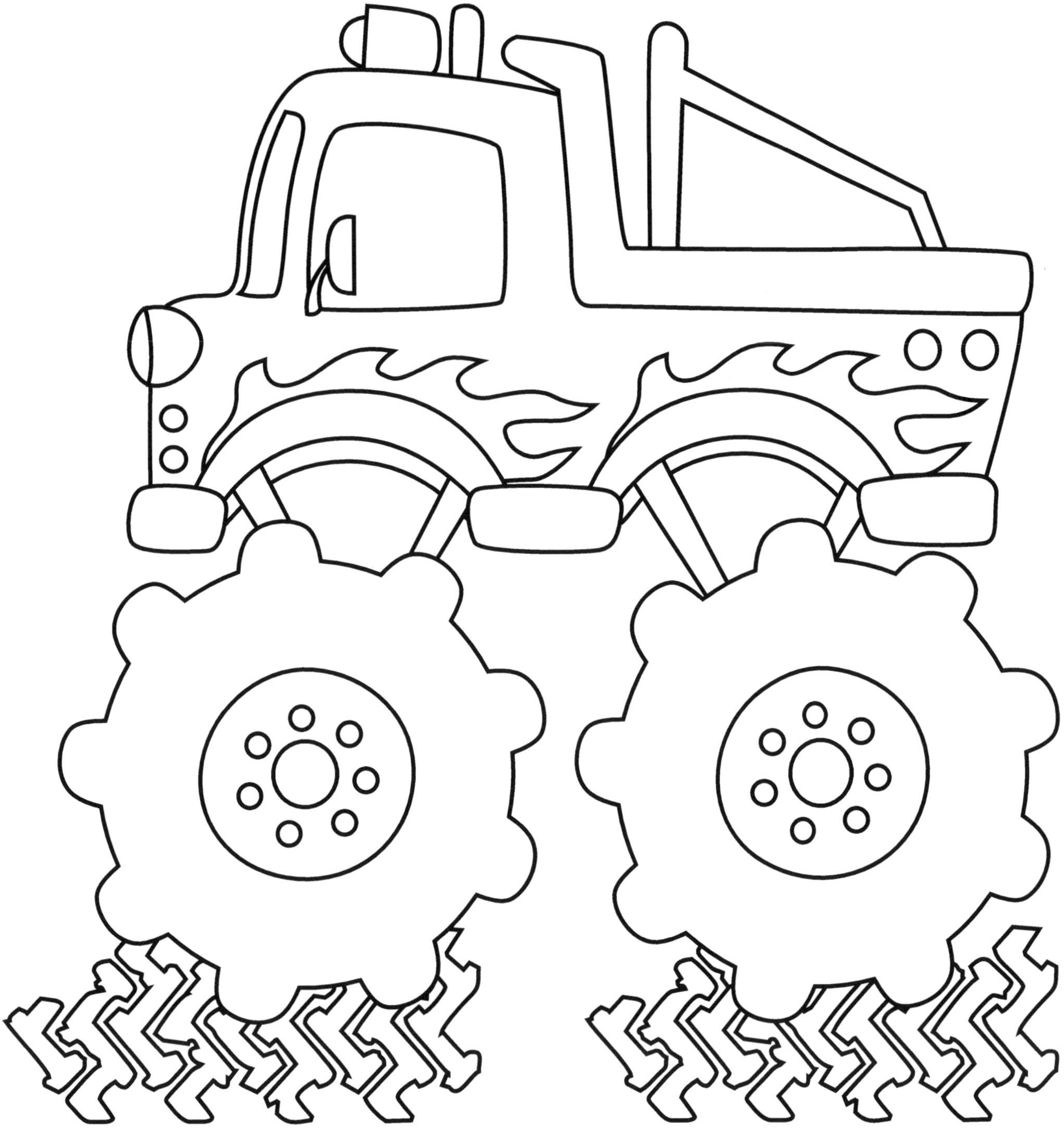

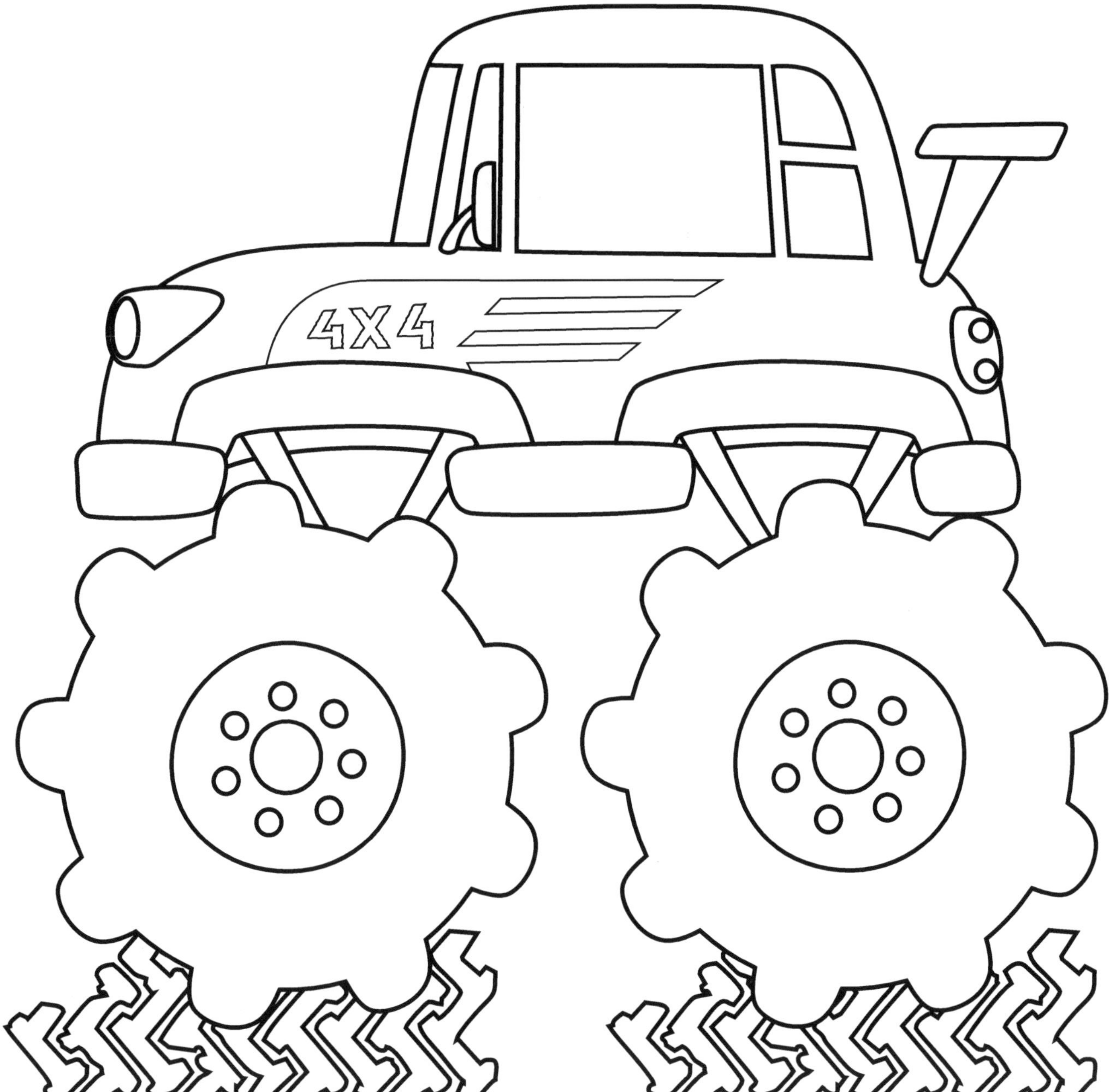
4X4

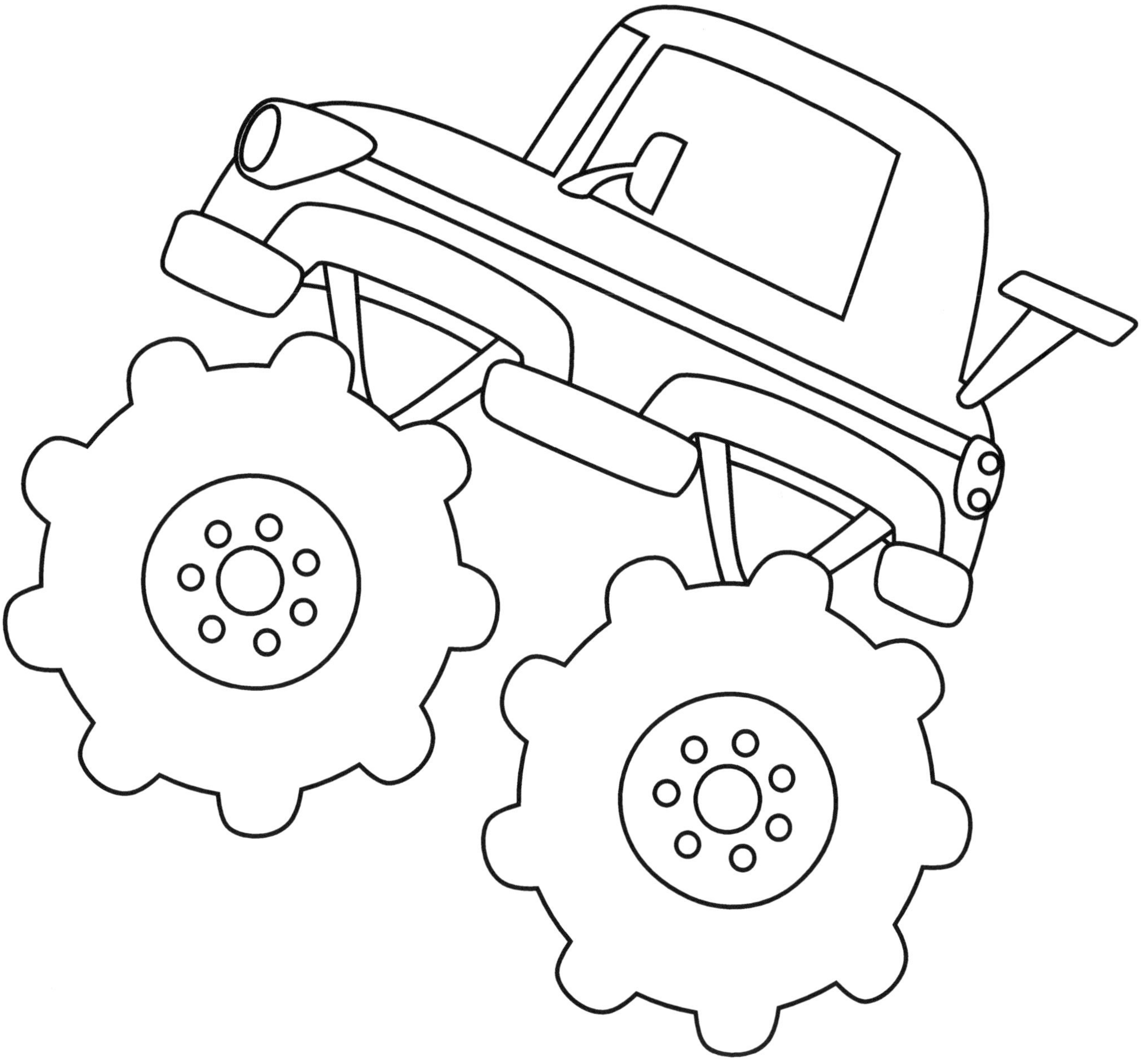

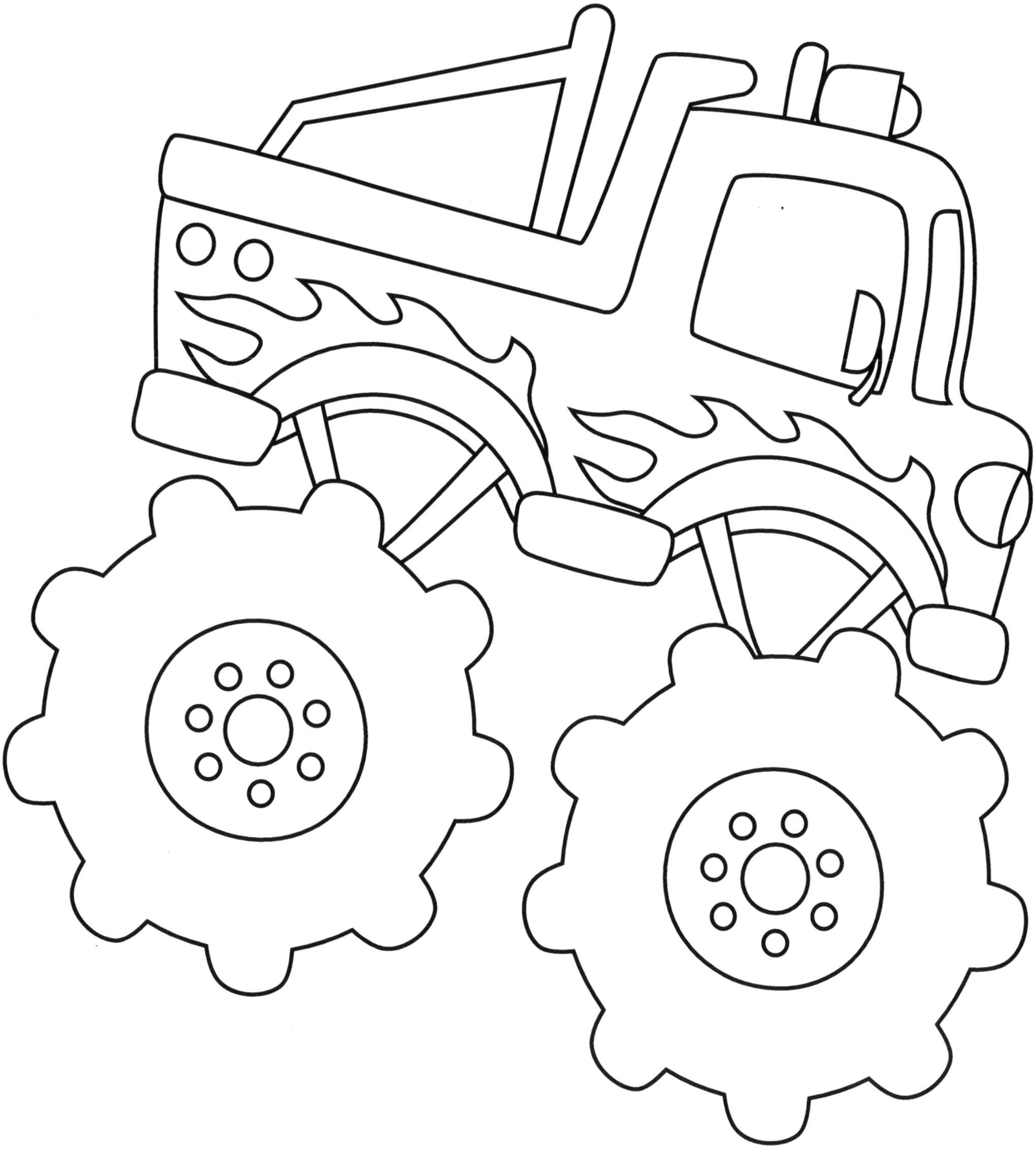

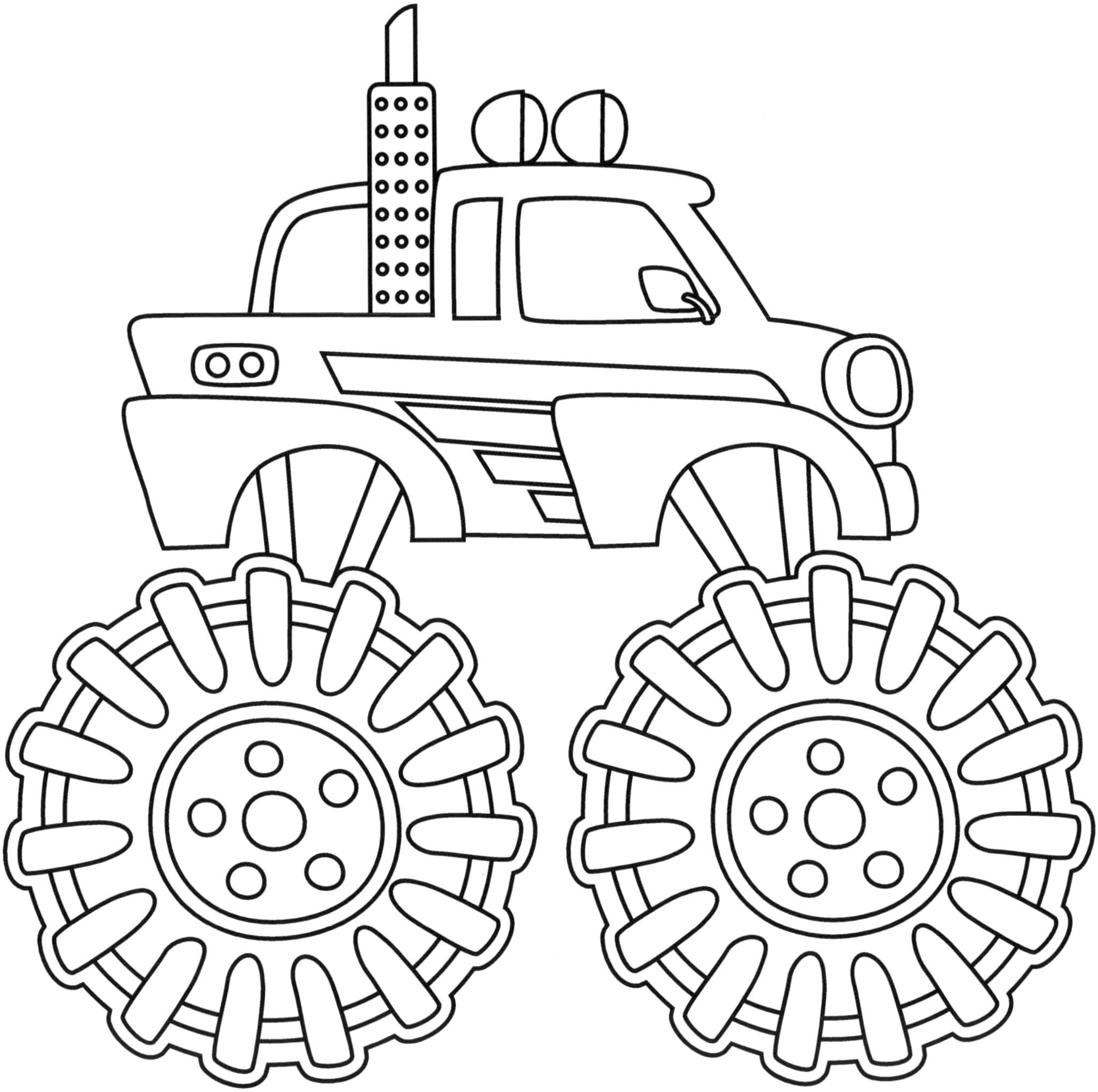

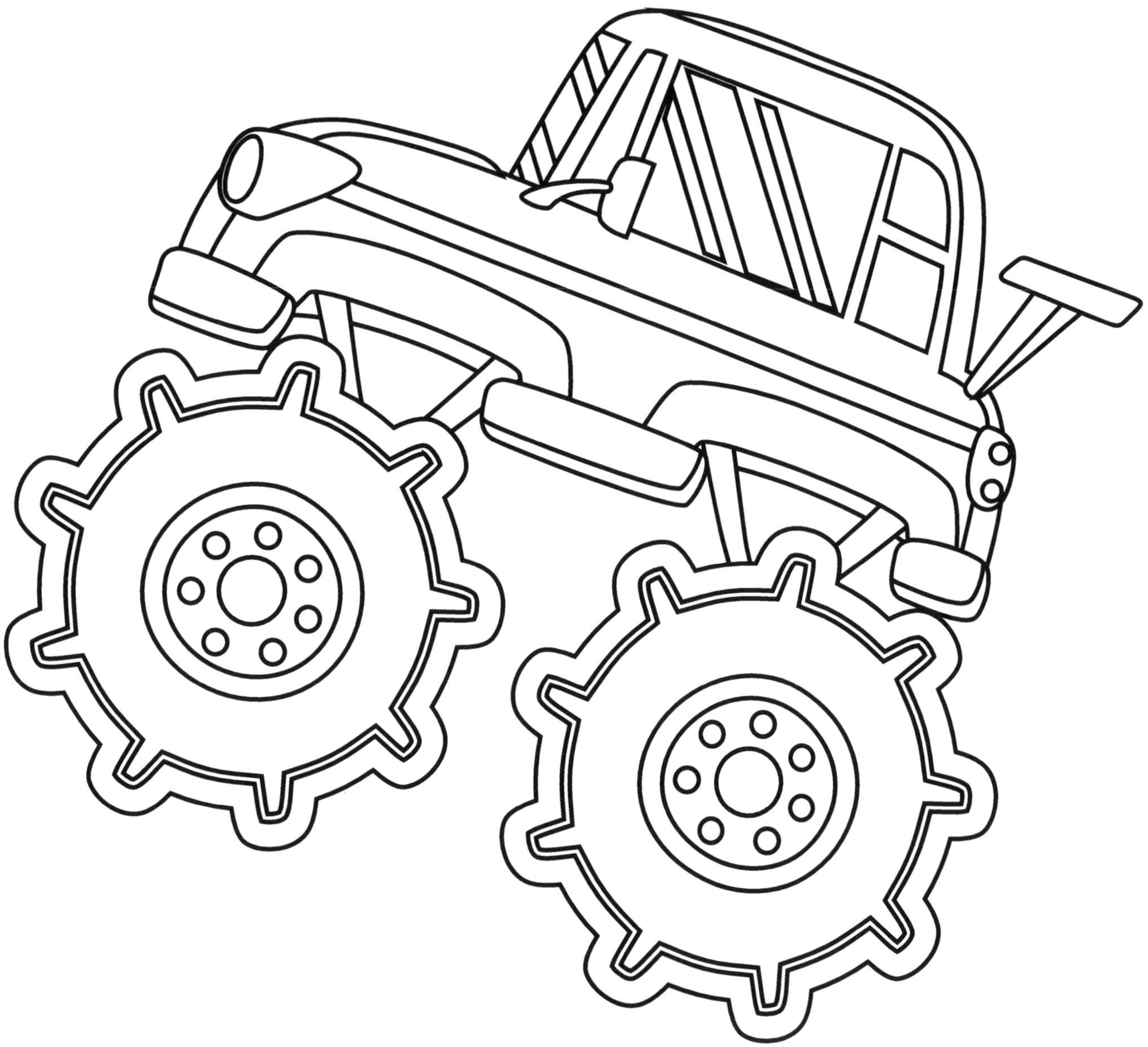

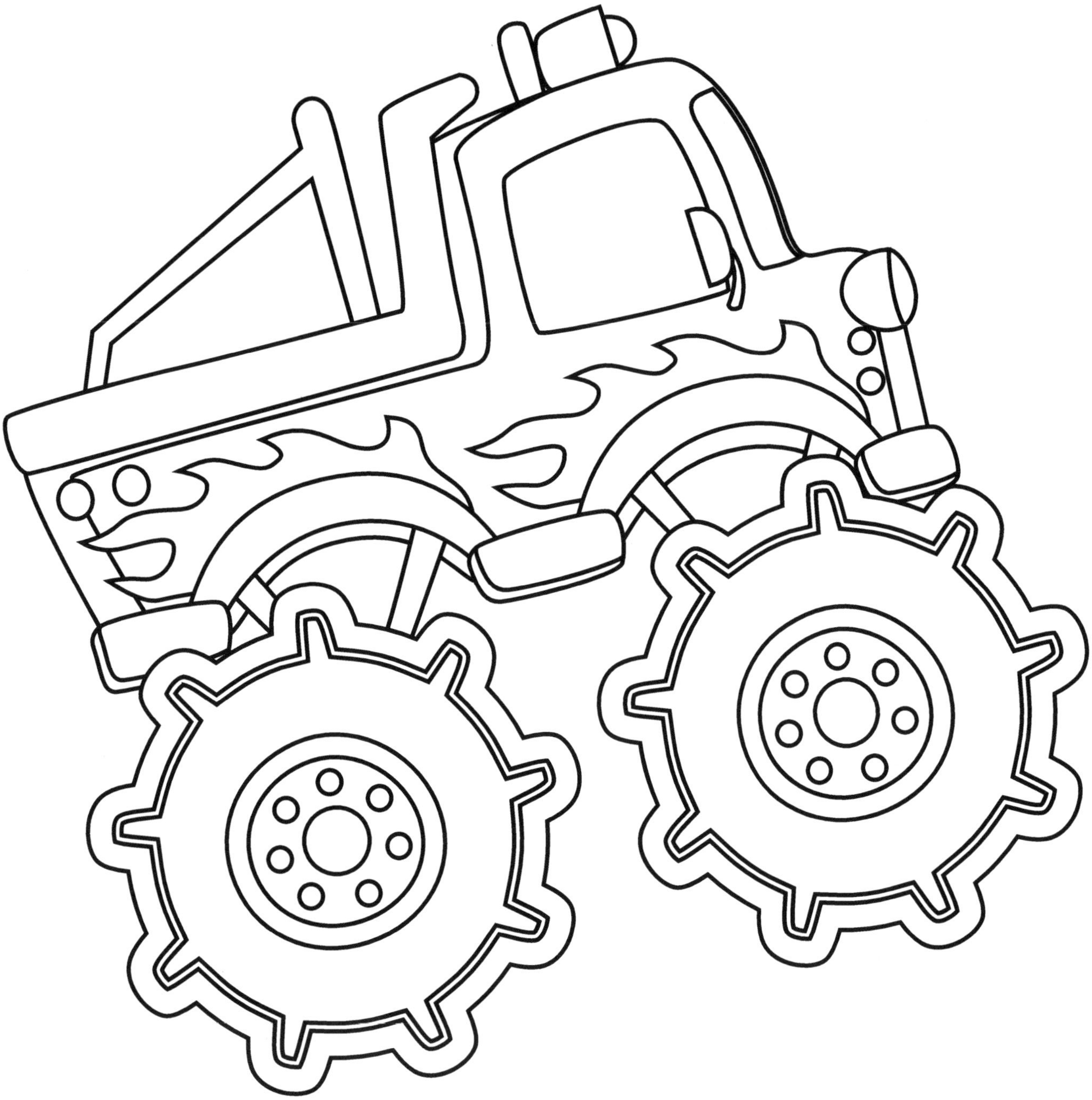

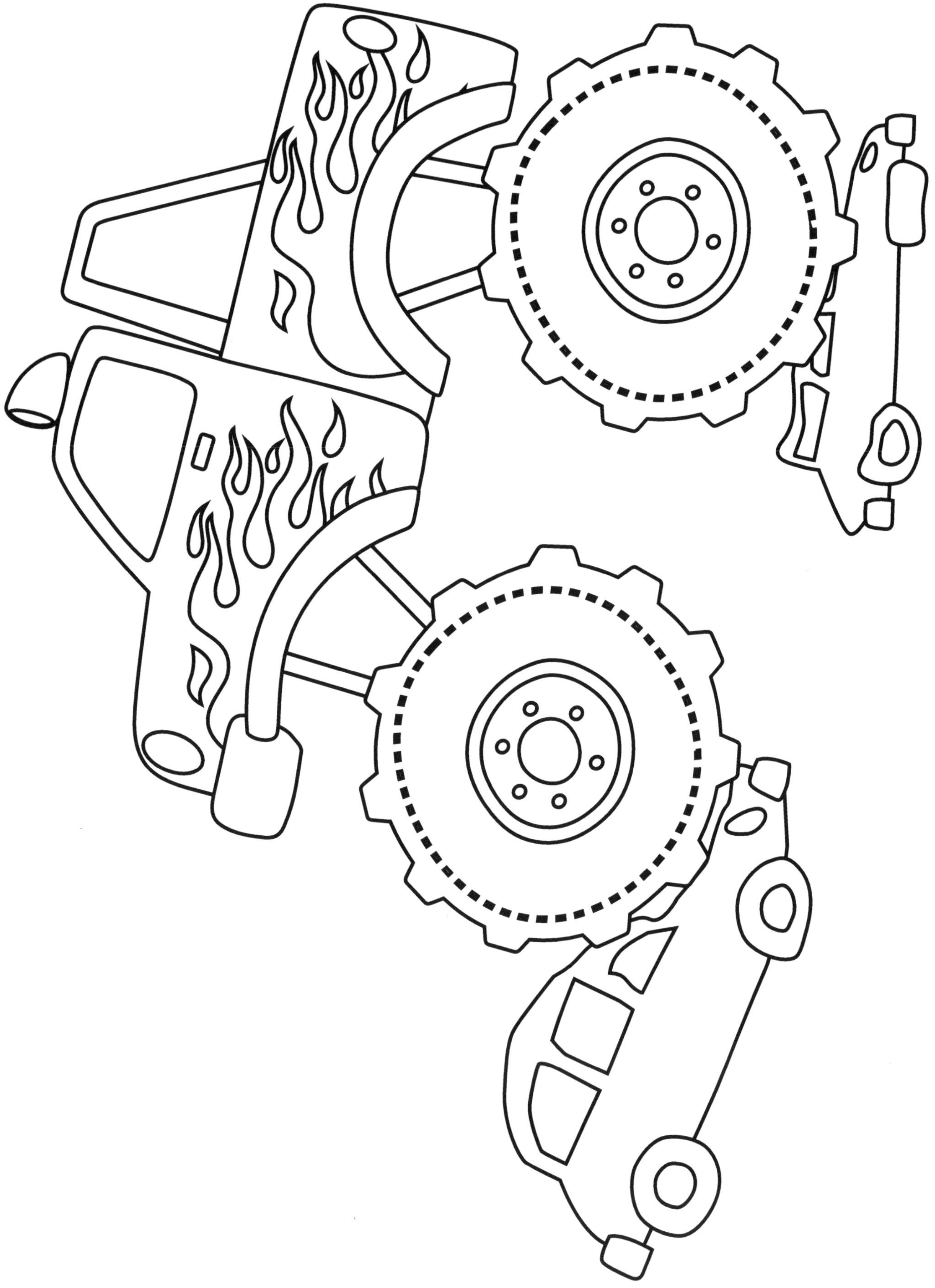

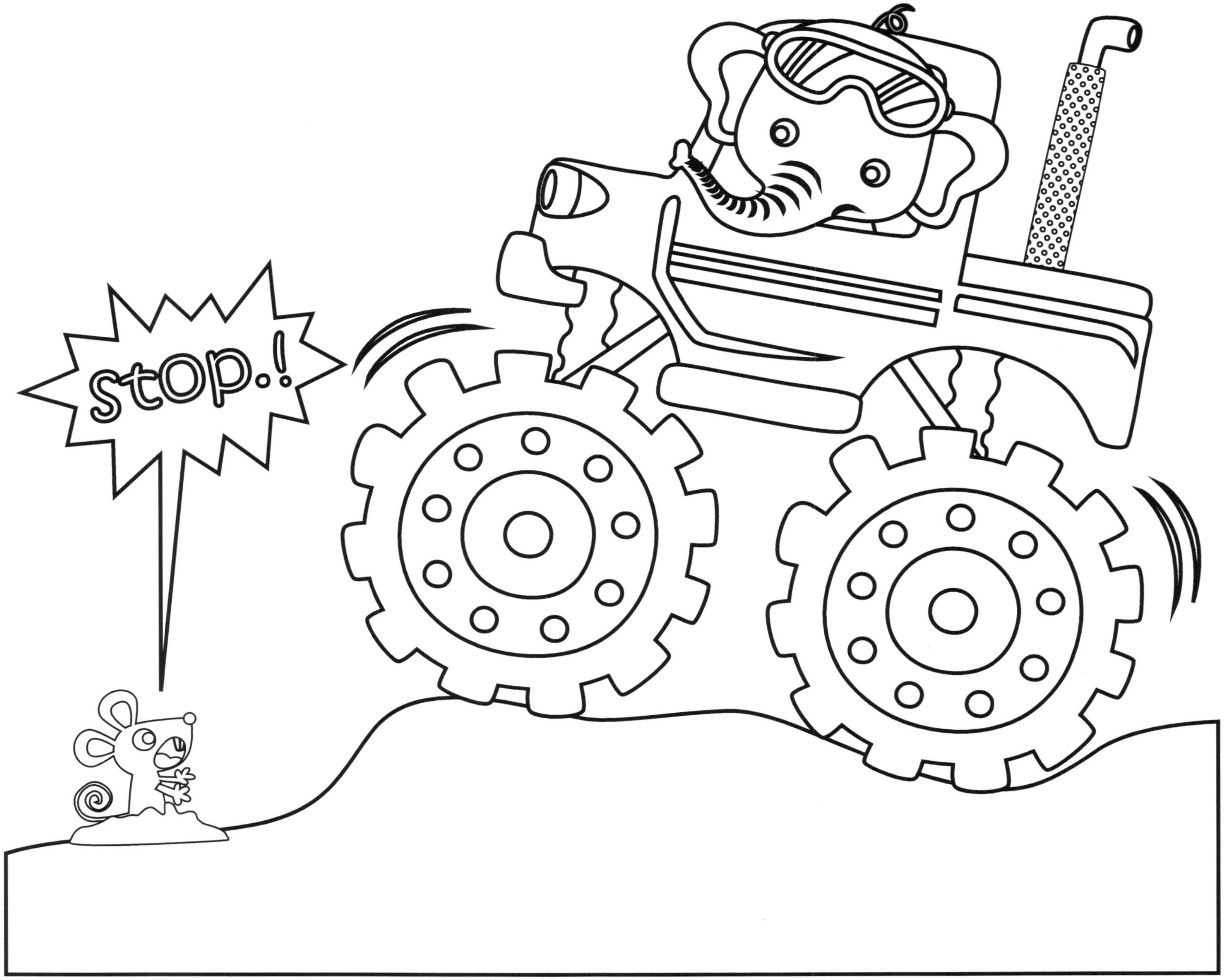
stop.!

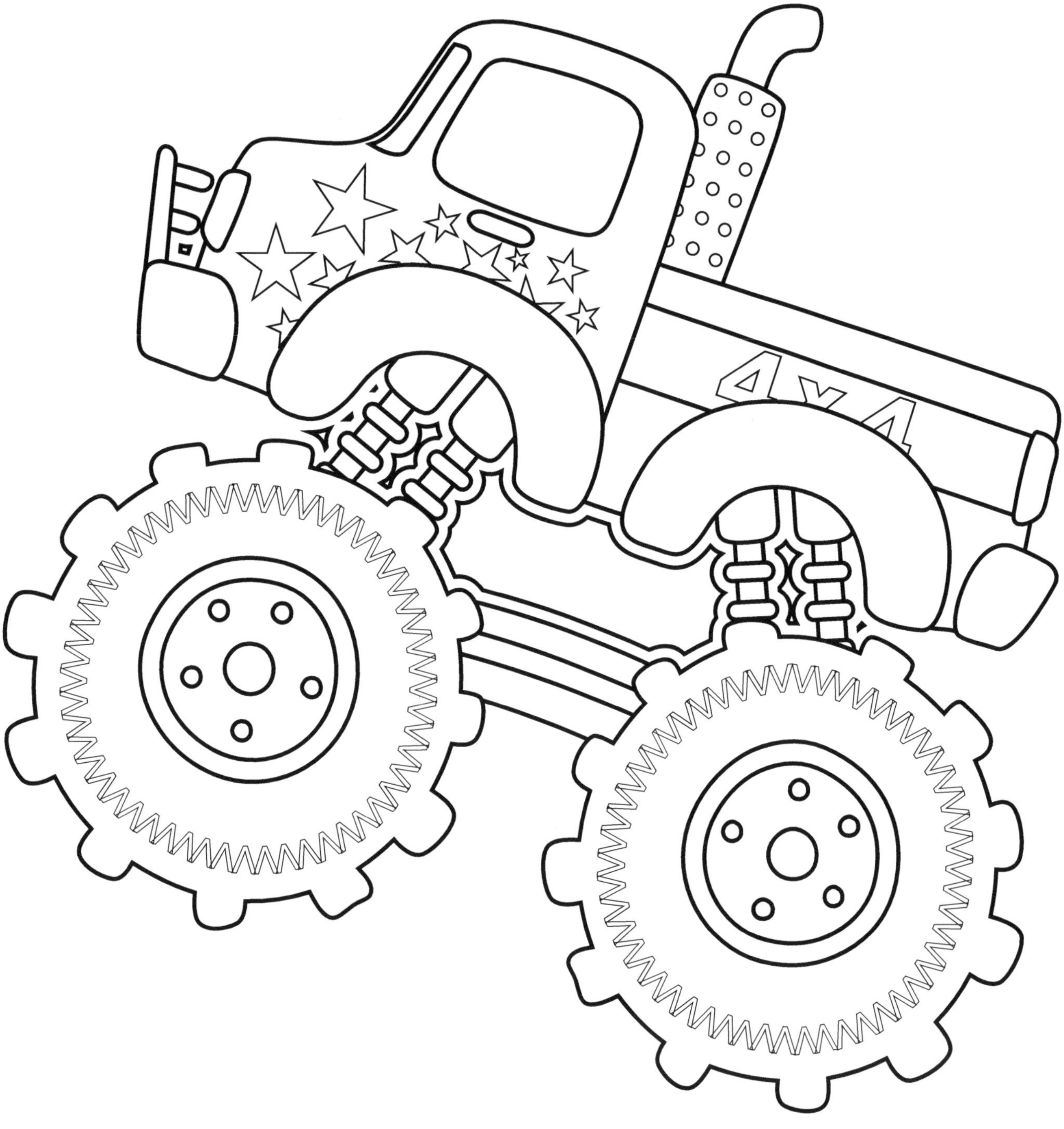
4x4

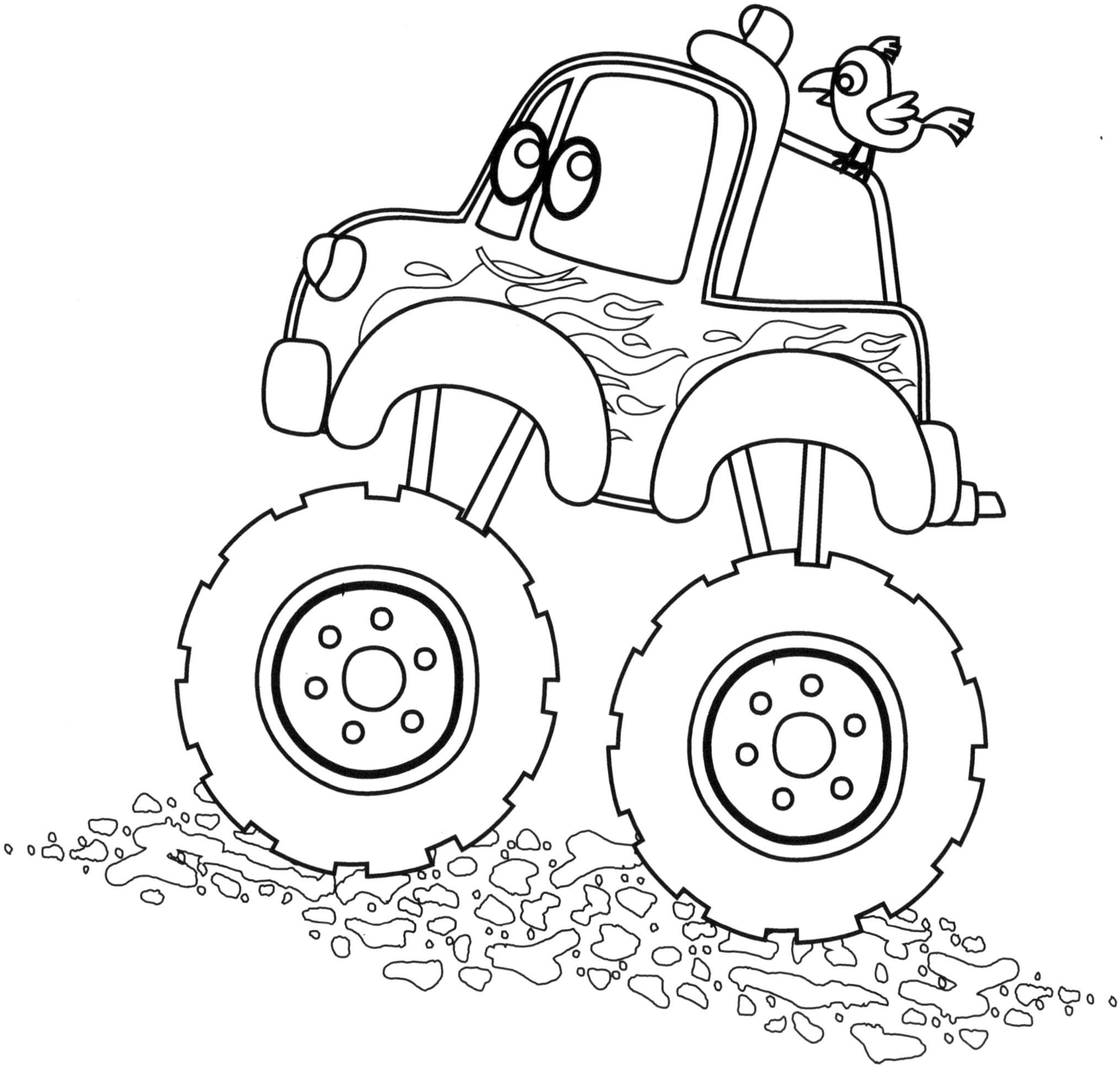

Made in the USA
Columbia, SC
25 September 2024

43047932R00030